D0548289

On Time
From Seasons to Split Seconds

The sun shines over Antarctica in late spring, seen in this time exposure photograph.

On Time

From Seasons to Split Seconds

By Gloria Skurzynski

NATIONAL GEOGRAPHIC SOCIETY

WASHINGTON, D.C.

In this 1,600-meter race, the winner crossed the finish line just one-third of a second ahead of the runner-up.

529
SKU
2000

As A BRAND-NEW BABY, you couldn't tell day from night. You cried whenever you were hungry. By the time you were two years old, you mostly slept through the dark hours and stayed awake during the daylight hours. At three, you understood that winter was different from summer. Winter meant snow and Santa Claus. By five, you knew when your birthday was coming—you could hardly wait! At the age of eight or nine, you'd already learned to tell time on all kinds of clocks and watches. By now, if you take part in sports, you've discovered the importance of a split second.

Your growing awareness of time, from your infancy to the age you are now, parallels the history of timekeeping on Earth. A hundred thousand years ago people didn't think much about time. They knew that the sun came up in the morning, giving them enough light to hunt for food. When the sun went down in the evening, it was too dark to see, so they went to sleep and waited for it to get light again. Then, as centuries went by....

 # Seasons

OBSERVANT PEOPLE began to notice that the sun rose in a slightly different place each day. When bears came out of their dens and birds started to nest, the early morning sun would appear at a particular spot on the horizon. Day by day, the place where the sun rose would move slightly farther north. By the time the days were warm and fruit grew on the trees, the point of sunrise had reached as far north as it was going to go—the "turning" point. From this point the sun reversed direction and began to move south again.

A supply of food had to be captured, cut, dried, and stored for the long, dark days of winter.

WINTER

SPRING

When snows were deep and people shivered in their caves, the sun rose as far south as it would ever reach—another turning point—and turned around to slowly head north again.

People became aware of this. That is, if they lived in the Northern Hemisphere. If they lived in the Southern Hemisphere, sunrise moved in the opposite direction —south in summer, north in winter.

In both hemispheres, the point where the sun came up changed with the seasons. And people remembered, because the same things happened again and again: When the sun rose *over there*, the rains would come and the river would flood. When the sun rose *right there*, animals would begin to migrate. That meant it was a good time to hunt.

What they didn't know was that from one sunrise to the next sunrise—one day—Earth spins around once on its axis.

Summer solstice,
about June 22

North Pole

South Pole

*Seasons change because
Earth doesn't stand straight up—it tilts.
In Earth's journey around the sun, if the Southern Hemisphere is
slanted toward the sun, it's summer there. At the same time,
it's winter in the Northern Hemisphere, which slants away from the sun.
Half a year later, the opposite is true. Also, because of the tilt of Earth's
axis and because its orbit isn't exactly circular, daylight
varies in length except at the equinoxes.*

8

SUMMER

FALL

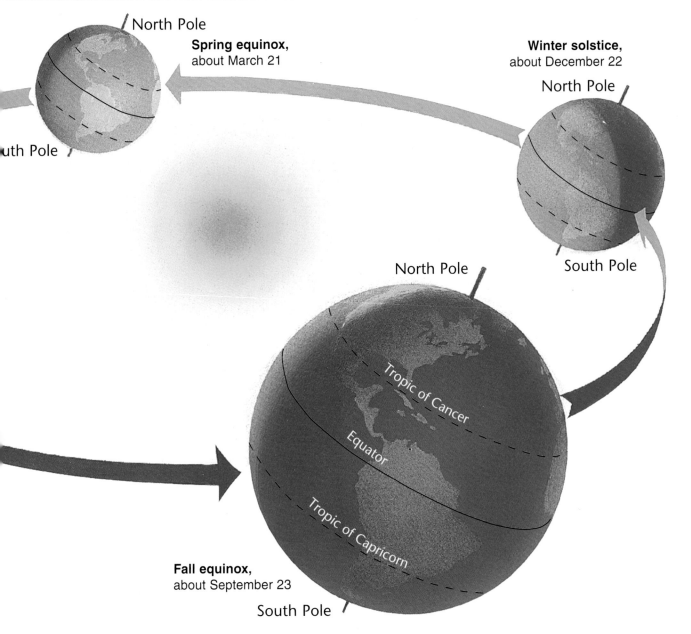

North Pole

Spring equinox,
about March 21

Winter solstice,
about December 22

North Pole

South Pole

North Pole

Tropic of Cancer

Equator

Tropic of Capricorn

South Pole

Fall equinox,
about September 23

South Pole

Nearly 4,000 years ago, on a southern plain called Stonehenge in the place we now know as England, people raised huge blocks of stone in a circle. The stones lined up with the sunrise at the summer solstice—the time when the sun rose as far north on the horizon as it would go—and at the winter solstice, when the sun rose as far south as it would go. It's thought that the alignment of the stones with the sun, moon, and stars predicted the seasons.

The axis of this ancient monument in England points toward sunrise on the morning of the summer solstice.

Years, Months, and Weeks

BEFORE STONEHENGE, Egyptian skywatchers had noticed that on a certain morning one particular star rose in a direct line with the sun. That star is the one we call Sirius, or the Dog Star; it's in the constellation Canis Major. From that morning until the next time Sirius rose with the sun, the Egyptians counted 365 days, or one year. Then everything started over again: seasons, the flooding of the Nile, the planting of crops. What they didn't know is that a year is the time it takes Earth to orbit once all the way around the sun, not exactly 365 days but 365 days, 5 hours, 48 minutes, and 46 seconds.

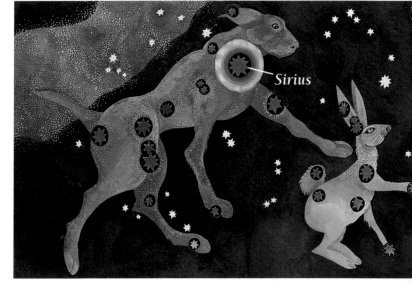

Ancient people imagined a dog in the constellation Canis Major.

Finding Sirius, the Dog Star, in the correct position could require the skill of an astronomer. But everyone can see the moon. By the light of the full moon, primitive people danced, prayed, and feasted. Best of all, that gleaming white circle in the night sky returned, like a promise from the gods, every 29½ days. How easy it was to count the passing of a month—people just waited for the next full moon!

But there was one very large problem with using the moon to mark the passage of time. You'll find more about this on page 17.

Why seven was chosen as the number of days in a week, no one really knows. It may have been because the moon enters a new phase—first quarter, full moon, last quarter, new moon—every seven days or so. Or perhaps it was because the Hebrew Bible taught that God created the world in six days, and rested on the seventh day, the Sabbath. More likely, seven was chosen thousands of years ago because the ancient Chaldeans, Mesopotamians, and Egyptians believed that seven

Like a huge sundial, the first built and largest of the Egyptian pyramids casts an evening shadow over modern-day Cairo.

heavenly bodies revolved around Earth: the sun, the moon, and the five known planets Mars, Mercury, Jupiter, Venus, and Saturn. They were wrong about the sun and planets revolving around Earth, but that wasn't discovered until much later.

The sun's day became Sunday; the moon's day became Monday. The next four days were named, many centuries later, for the Norse gods Tiw (Tuesday), Woden (Wednesday), Thor (Thursday), and Frigg (Friday). Only Saturday kept its planet's name—in honor of Saturn.

 # Hours

PEOPLE NOTICED their own shadows changing direction as the sun moved across the sky. So did the shadows of trees, rocks, and sticks in the ground. When the sun rose in the east in the morning, shadows stretched out toward the west. As morning wore on, the shadows got shorter, until at noon, they hardly showed at all. In the afternoon, the shadows pointed east, growing longer and longer until the sun set.

The Egyptians, and later the Romans, always divided daylight into 12 equal parts they called "hours." Although the Babylonians are believed to be the people who invented sundials to measure the journey of the sun across the sky, ancient Egyptians, too, built very large sundials—tall, slender, four-sided monuments called obelisks. At the base of the obelisks, they put marks for hours. As an obelisk's shadow crept toward each mark, one after the other, a passerby could tell the time. In Egypt and Rome, the sundials would have been fairly accurate, because close to the Equator days and nights are nearly equal all year long. But farther north or south, days and nights are equal *only* at the spring and fall equinoxes (March 20 or 21 and September 22 or 23); the word "equinox" means "equal night." For the rest of the year, daylight and darkness are not equal to each other.

At Stonehenge, for instance, on the shortest day of the year (the winter solstice), less than 8 hours of daylight is measured between sunrise and sunset. On the longest day of the year (the summer solstice), daylight lasts about 16 hours and 40 minutes. So dividing daylight into 12 equal parts would mean that, at Stonehenge, an hour at the winter solstice would last only two-thirds as long as an hour at the equinoxes. And an hour at the summer solstice would last one-third longer than at the equinoxes.

Water clocks were better, because they worked even when clouds covered the sun, or at night after the sun had set. Simple water clocks had been used almost as long as sundials. Water would be poured into a bowl that had a small hole in the bottom. As the water dripped out, its level sank, revealing lines marked on the inside of the bowl. Each new line that came into sight meant an hour had passed. After the bowl emptied, someone had to fill it again to start all over.

TOWER OF THE WINDS

ABOUT 50 B.C., when the Roman Empire ruled Greece, a Macedonian astronomer named Andronikos built the complex, octagon-shaped Tower of the Winds. Each of its eight outer walls held a sundial. Inside the tower stood an instrument for telling time on cloudy days: a water clock.

The sea god Poseidon, holding his three-pronged trident, stood guard over the Tower of the Winds. But a human attendant had to drain the water tank every 24 hours in order to reset the time. Scientists think it worked this way: Pipes carried water from a spring into a basin holding a float. As the water rose, a chain from the float turned a bronze disk that pointed out the hours. This ingenious clock was called a *horologion*, meaning an "hour indicator."

ONE OF
THE TOWER'S
EIGHT
SUNDIALS

CUTAWAY

CITIZEN
OBSERVES
TIME

WATER RESERVOIR

*The Tower of the Winds told time two ways: by water and by sun. As the days passed,
shadows from the spikes on all eight sides of the tower marked the hours.*

 # Calendars

WEEKS AND HOURS are divisions of time created by humans and abided by because most everyone agrees to go along with the arrangement. Weeks *could* be 8 days or 10 days long—and in other times and places, they have been. There's no real reason for days to be divided into 24 hours; 15 or 20 would do just as well, as long as everyone was willing to follow the same system.

Years, months, and days are different. They're Earth's natural timekeeping units. A day can be reckoned from one sunrise to the next: what we call 24 hours. A year can be counted from one summer solstice to the next: 365¼ days. And a lunar month lasts from one full moon to the next—29½ days. But a lunar month and a calendar month are two different things, and this is why: If you divide 365¼ days by 29½ days, you get twelve months—with 11¼ days left over. Those extra days gave early calendar makers major problems. To use lunar months in a solar calendar (solar referring to the sun) meant adding a day here and there to come up with a total of 365 days from solstice to solstice. Sometimes whole months were added to keep the calendar in sync with the seasons.

Some calendars didn't rely on the moon at all: The Aztec people of Mexico designed a calendar that had 18 months of 20 days each, totaling 360 days. To get to 365, they added 5 days and celebrated those days with sacrifices to the gods. Human sacrifice.

But most calendars used 12 months, although the months weren't the same length within a calendar. In our calendar, February is just 28 days long (29 in leap years). Four of our months have 30 days, and seven have 31 days.

The Aztecs carved their ideas about time and the heavens onto a 12-foot-wide stone called the Sun Stone. Each of the 20 days in the Aztec month had its own sign. Starting at the top center of the middle ring and going counterclockwise, the signs (each in its own square) are: 1. crocodile, 2. wind, 3. house, 4. lizard, 5. serpent, 6. death, 7. deer, 8. rabbit, 9. water, 10. dog, 11. monkey, 12. grass, 13. reed, 14. jaguar, 15. eagle, 16. vulture, 17. movement, 18. flint knife, 19. rain, 20. flower.

The names of months in our calendar come from the Roman calendar at the time of Julius Caesar. Their year began in March. The twelve months were called Martius, Aprilis, Maius, Junius, Quintilis, Sextilis, September, October, November, December, Januarius, Februarius.

Quintilis? Sextilis? Those names didn't last, because the emperor Julius Caesar wanted a month named after him. He replaced Quintilis with Julius. Then his successor, Augustus, demanded a month of his own and changed Sextilis to Augustus. Can you match those two months and the other Roman months to the names we use today?

In 46 B.C., Julius Caesar reformed the calendar into 12 months totaling 365 days, with a leap day every fourth year to take care of the extra quarter days. That still didn't work out perfectly. (An extra day every leap year makes each year too long by 11 minutes and 14 seconds.)

 Points In Time

Julius Caesar, shown on this Roman coin, named a month after himself.

THE ABBREVIATIONS "B.C." AND "A.D." divide our calendar into events that happened before the birth of Christ—B.C.— or after—A.D., which stands for "anno Domini," Latin for "the year of the Lord." Actually, Jesus was probably born about four years before A.D. 1.

Many people take dates very seriously, even though dates are only man-made systems invented to keep track of time. In 1582, Pope Gregory XIII reformed the calendar to account for all those 11-minute surpluses that had added up through the centuries. The British stuck with the old Julian calendar until the year 1752. By then, the Julian calendar was 11 days out of whack.

To fix it, the British government decreed that September 14 would follow September 2 in the year 1752. September's calendar dates would then read 1, 2, 14, 15, 16, and so on. At this news, people rioted in the streets and stoned the carriage of the prime minister, howling, "Give us

Special calendar dates like a millennium set off huge celebrations worldwide.

back our 11 days." They believed their lives had somehow been shortened by the changing dates on the calendar. Of course, that wasn't true at all: They lived just as long as they would have if the calendar had stayed the same.

Numbers like A.D. 1000 and A.D. 2000 cause a lot of excitement. On both those dates, a few worriers predicted that the world would end, and others celebrated joyously. It didn't matter that the date January 1, A.D. 2000 had come from centuries of calendar adjustment or that other calendars have other dates for A.D. 2000: 5760 in the Hebrew calendar; 2056 in the Hindu; 1420 A.H. in the Islamic calendar. According to the Julian calendar, January 1, 2000 fell on December 19, 1999. The Aztec calendar called it Ehecatl, day of the wind (page 16). There was nothing magical about January 1, 2000.

If a year is the time it takes a planet to swing once around the sun, then a Martian year is 687 days long (in Earth days); a year on Jupiter lasts 11.9 Earth years; and Pluto's year drags on for 248 years, reckoned in Earth time.

ALBUQUERQUE ACADEMY LIBRARY

 Heavenly Bodies

REAL TIME—nature's time—relates to the movements of heavenly bodies: Earth, sun, moon and stars. From earliest times, astronomers studied the heavens to track these movements. As they counted days, months, and years, they kept records of the positions of sun, moon, and stars in the heavens. Thousands of years ago, Chinese astronomers saw five planets clustered together, "lined up like a string of pearls." This sighting was so rare that the Chinese chose it to be the first day of their calendar: March 5, 1953 B.C., by our reckoning.

Navigators have always studied the positions of the stars, and have steered their ships by watching the movements of those stars. Mathematicians and astronomers noted celestial positions precisely; their records were studied century after century by other astronomers, who learned to predict, with reasonable accuracy, the eclipses of the sun and the moon.

Although hourglasses could measure portions of hours fairly well, ordinary people didn't worry about small units of time. They worked from sunrise to sunset and went to bed soon after the sun was gone, whether it was summer or winter.

But in 1543, a revolution in science took place, changing our understanding of the way the universe works. Nicolaus Copernicus, a Polish churchman and mathematician, quietly reported to an unbelieving world that Earth is not the center of the universe, that the sun does not orbit

For thousands of years, people believed that Earth stood at the center of the universe, and that the sun, moon, stars, planets, and comets revolved around us.

Christopher Columbus and The Moon Eclipse

ON THE FOURTH VOYAGE of Christopher Columbus across the Atlantic, his ships became so worm-eaten that they were no longer safe to sail. For many months, Columbus and his crew were stranded at the place now called Haiti. While they waited to be rescued, the native Indians brought them food.

Because of the rocking and sometimes violent motion of the waves, ships could not use pendulum clocks. Ship captains relied on sandglasses like this, an exact duplicate of one used by Christopher Columbus.

After a while the natives got tired of this and refused to supply the crew any longer. Worried that his men would starve, Columbus thought of a way to trick the natives. He owned a book about celestial mechanics— the motions of the sun, moon, and stars. Checking it, Columbus saw that an eclipse of the moon was due to happen in a few days.

If the Indians didn't bring him food, Columbus threatened, he would ask his God to take away the moon. The natives scoffed at this. But exactly when Columbus predicted it would, the moon began to disappear. After the frightened Indians promised to give him all the food he needed, Columbus agreed to bring back the moon. He told them exactly when it would reappear, and he was right. The moon came back. Columbus had timed the eclipse with a sandglass. We call it an hourglass.

This 16th-century woodcut asked the question "If a man broke through the sphere of the stars, what would he find on the other side?"

Earth, but that each year our Earth goes once around the sun, which stands still at the center of our solar system. *This* was an incredible discovery! It shook the world. People's reactions ranged from amazement to anger—mostly anger, because the Copernican theory meant that humans were not at the center of creation. From then on skywatchers knew Earth's real location when they calculated time by the heavenly bodies.

 # Mechanical Clocks

THE REVOLUTION IN SCIENCE began to gain momentum. In 1581 a teenager named Galileo Galilei attended services in a cathedral in Pisa, Italy. (The famous Leaning Tower is the bell tower of that cathedral.) There Galileo watched a lamp swinging from a chain attached to the high ceiling. It seemed to him that whether the lamp swung in a big wide arc or swung in a narrower arc, each oscillation (swing) took the same amount of time. To test this, he used his own pulse to count how long each swing lasted.

Later, Galileo experimented with pendulums enough to prove that his ideas about the swinging lamp were correct. He designed a simple pendulum clock, but he never built it.

At the time of Galileo, mechanical clocks had been invented, but they measured only hours, not minutes. The first mechanical clocks had a weight fastened to a rope wrapped a few times around a revolving drum. When the weight sank slowly (because a counterweight was at the other end of the rope), it triggered a hammer that struck a bell to announce the hour. The word for bell is *clocca* in Latin, *glocke* in German; *cloche* in French, *clocke* in Middle Dutch, and *clok* in Middle English. These clocks could be wrong by as much as an hour a day.

When bells toll the hours on the Prague Astronomical Clock in the Czech Republic, figures of the Twelve Apostles move across the two high windows.

Gears with teeth interrupted the fall of the driving weight, one cog at a time—catch and release, catch and release. Time no longer flowed smoothly as it had with sun shadows, water clocks, and sandglasses. Now it ticked.

Days could now be divided into 24 equal hours, whether summer or winter. Clocks now had hands. Even though they weren't too accurate, clocks were installed in the church bell towers of cities. They announced the "hours" to the townspeople by ringing bells. Some of these clocks had mechanical figures that not only struck the hour but jousted or paraded or danced.

Minutes and Seconds

LIKE WEEKS AND HOURS, minutes and seconds are man-made divisions of time. This system of time probably came from those same ancient Babylonians who invented sundials. They divided day into twelve equal parts, divided these parts into 60 smaller parts, and divided those into 60 still smaller parts. The Romans called the largest part *horo* (we say "hour"); the next part *pars minuta prima* (we say "minute"); and the smallest division *pars minuta secunda* (we say "second"). For most of the history of the human race, however, minutes and seconds just didn't matter much.

Then, in 1656, a Dutch scientist named Christiaan Huygens added to Galileo's ideas for an oscillating (swinging) pendulum and made the first pendulum clock. It was accurate to within one minute a day. Soon he made one that told time correctly to within ten seconds a day.

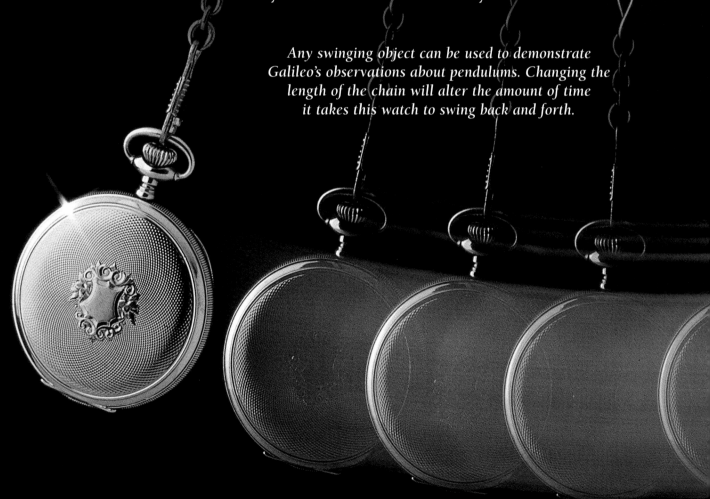

Any swinging object can be used to demonstrate Galileo's observations about pendulums. Changing the length of the chain will alter the amount of time it takes this watch to swing back and forth.

Navigation

CLOCKS DIDN'T WORK WELL ON SHIPS because the tossing and swaying of the high seas disrupted their mechanisms. Then in 1761 a carpenter and self-taught clockmaker named John Harrison built a chronometer (ship's clock) that was stable enough to withstand rough seas. This was important because navigators needed accurate timekeeping to locate their positions on the high seas.

By the 19th century, most of the world's sailing ships used sea charts that listed Greenwich, England, as the "prime meridian." That means zero degrees longitude—the imaginary line from the North Pole to the South Pole—runs through Greenwich. If navigators aboard ships had clocks that told them exactly what time it was at Greenwich, and they checked the positions of the sun and moon and stars where they were—and if they had reliable sea charts that told them where the celestial (heavenly) bodies were *supposed* to be—they could pretty well get a fix on their locations.

Not until the 18th century did clocks become stable enough to work on a pitching, rolling sea.

Lines of longitude—called *meridians*—are like rubber bands stretched around a ball, criss-crossing to a single point at the top (North Pole) and at the bottom (South Pole) but spread out at the middle (the Equator). The greatest distance between one degree of longitude and the next—about 69 miles—is at the Equator. Maps and globes show Earth divided by meridians that are 15 degrees apart (see pages 30–31). Each 15-degree section marks how far the sun travels in one hour, or *looks like* it's traveling, since we know that the sun stands still and it's Earth that rotates on its axis. Twenty-four hours times 15 degrees is 360 degrees, the circumference of a circle and of a sphere like Earth. Earth rotates on its axis a full 360 degrees in 24 hours.

 # Standard Time

ALMOST EVERY CITY AND TOWN on Earth used to have its own local time. Clocks were set when the sun stood directly overhead at noon. From one city to another, time didn't match up. In the 1800s, when it was two in the afternoon in San Francisco, California, the clocks in Sacramento, 90 miles to the east, said 3 minutes and 56 seconds past two.

Then the railroads came, and people could travel hundreds of miles in a day. Trying to figure out a railroad schedule when every city followed its own time was almost impossible. Someone traveling from Boston to Washington would have to reset his watch five times during the trip and hope that his watch was reliable. Railroad conductors and engineers were supposed to know the exact time. When they didn't, their mistakes could lead to confusion—or disaster!

At noon on Sunday, November 18, 1883, standard time was adopted in the United States and Canada. Although Greenwich, England, had been used on maps and charts as the prime meridian since the late 1700s, the designation didn't become official until October 13, 1884. Standard time meant that when it was noon at the city of Greenwich, England, it would be 11 a.m. 15 degrees to the west, 10 a.m. 15 degrees west of that, and so on, halfway around Earth. Moving east, it would be 1 p.m. 15 degrees from Greenwich, 2 p.m. 15 degrees farther east, and so on.

"Go to Thunder…"

ON APRIL 19, 1891, a mail train called Number Four was traveling east toward Cleveland, Ohio, going fast. On the same track, another train was heading west. The engineer and the conductor of the westbound train had received written orders to let the mail train pass theirs. Farther down the line, they got another warning when a telegraph operator ran toward their train and shouted, "Be careful! Number Four is on time."

"Go to Thunder! I know my business," the conductor shouted back. He looked at his watch, which was accurate. But he didn't check his watch against the engineer's, and the engineer's watch happened to be four minutes slow.

Near a tiny station called Kipton, the westbound engineer looked out in horror to see Mail Train Number Four bearing down on him, full speed ahead. He threw on his brakes, but it was too late. In the crash, the engineers of both trains were killed, along with nine other people. After that disaster, all railroads adopted universal timekeeping standards. Conductors were required to have their watches checked every three months by approved watch repairmen and to carry signed notes as proof. From then on, railroad watches kept accurate time to within 30 seconds per week.

No cheap pocket watches for railroad employees! For greatest accuracy, they needed watches with jeweled movements.

Sea travel created the need for lines of longitude. Railroad travel created the need for standard time.

INTERNATIONAL TIME ZONES

1 a.m. 2 a.m. 3 a.m. 4 a.m. 5 a.m. 6 a.m. 7 a.m. 8 a.m. 9 a.m. 10 a.m. 11 a.m. 12 noon 1 p.m. 2 p.m. 3 p.m. 4 p.m. 5 p.m. 6 p.m. 7 p.m. 8 p.m. 9 p.m. 10 p.m. 11 p.m. 12 midnight

Greenwich, England

Europe

Asia

North America

8:30 am

3:30 pm

4:30 pm

6:30 pm

Africa

5:30 pm

South America

Fiji

10:30 pm

Australia

9:30 pm

Prime Mer

Date Line

When it's high noon in Greenwich, it's midnight in Fiji. The colors on the time zone map match the meridians on which they are centered (shown on globe).

12 noon

1 p.m.

2 p.m.

3 p.m.

4 p.m.

5 p.m

The prime meridian runs north and south through the *middle* of Greenwich's time zone. The line of longitude that defines each time zone, whether it's 30 degrees or 75 degrees or 105 degrees or more (all time zone meridians can be divided by 15), lies in the center of the time zone, not at the edges.

Many time zone boundaries were drawn crooked in order to keep an entire country inside a single time zone so that all its cities would be on the same time. In some states of the United States (but not all of them), time zone boundaries were set so that a state wouldn't be sliced apart and be in different time zones. Russia is so vast it has 11 different time zones. China, also vast, uses only one time zone—eight hours later than Greenwich.

INDIAN OCEAN

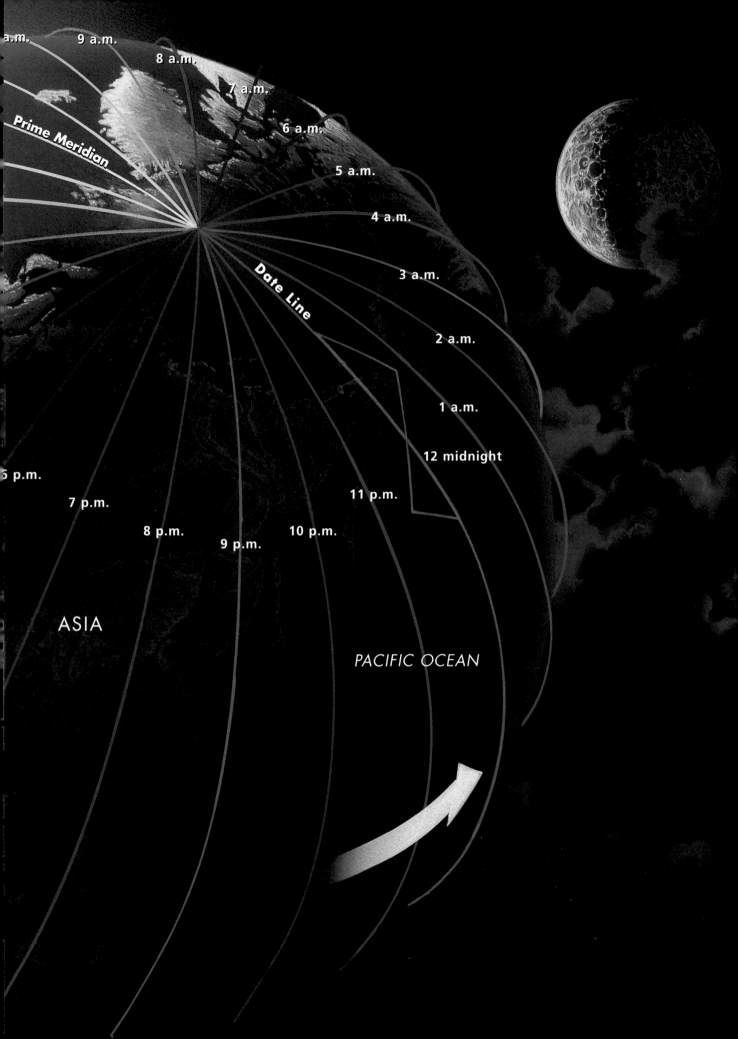

Split Seconds

DURING WORLD WAR I, soldiers under fire in the trenches didn't have time to pull out pocket watches. To help them, the Ingersoll Watch Company soldered wires onto pocket watches, above the 12 and below the 6, and ran a strap through the wires. That's how the wristwatch was born. Soon everybody wore one.

Seconds were being split into smaller and smaller fractions. Remember Galileo and the oscillation (swinging) of the cathedral lamp? Today, the oscillations of quartz crystals in digital watches keep time to a thousandth of a second per day. That's called a millisecond. Other fragments of seconds are:

This cesium cylinder will be part of an atomic clock that's accurate to within one nanosecond a day.

- **MICROSECOND** — a millionth of a second
- **NANOSECOND** — a billionth of a second
- **PICOSECOND** — a trillionth of a second
- **FEMTOSECOND** — a thousandth of a picosecond

How many times can you split a second? Infinitely. There's no limit. Who needs to do this? Scientists.

In physics experiments, the short lifetime of some particles has been measured at one one-hundred-millionth of a second, and others at as brief a time as a millionth of a billionth of a billionth of a second. Scientists need clocks that can count tiny fractions of seconds.

A vibrating atom is an ideal type of clock. Electrons of atoms oscillate with a rhythm so regular that it never changes— not a million years ago, not a million years from now, not in a galaxy far, far away. Today's atomic clocks are tuned to the frequency of oscillations of one particular kind of atom—the cesium atom (cesium is a silvery white metal). One second is now defined as 9,192,631,770 oscillations of the cesium atom.

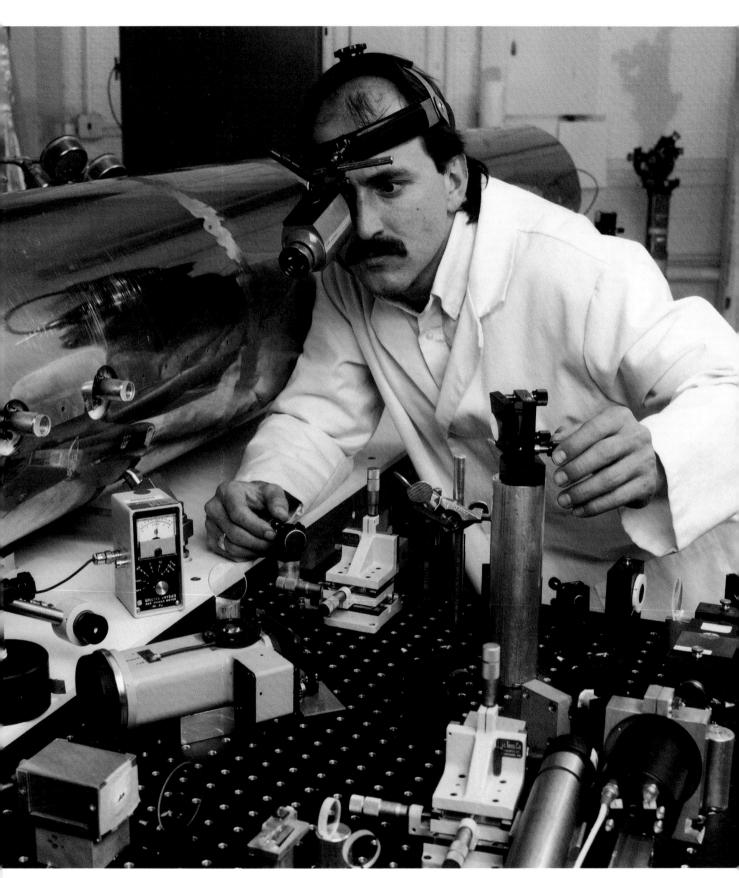

At the National Institute of Standards and Technology in Boulder, Colorado, cesium atomic clocks keep time accurately to within one second in ten million years.

$E = mc^2$

Albert Einstein (1879–1955) didn't talk until he was 3 years old.
But all during his childhood he showed a brilliant curiosity about the world
around him. When he was 12, he taught himself geometry. When he was 26,
he changed our understanding of the universe.

# Space-Time

EVEN DISTANCE can be measured by time. If you're not used to the metric system, you may think of a meter as being 39.37 inches long. At one time, a standard meter was the distance between two lines on a platinum bar stored near Paris, France. Today, a meter is defined as the distance light travels, in a vacuum, in one 299,792,458th of a second—that's 186,282 miles in a whole second. That's fast! This is known as the speed of light, and it's usually rounded off to 186,000 miles per second. At the National Institute of Standards and Technology and NASA's Jet Propulsion Laboratory, researchers are working on a laser-cooled cesium atomic clock to be placed aboard the International Space Station. The space clock will help test whether the speed of light is the same in all directions.

In one year, light travels about six trillion miles. That's called a light-year, a unit used to measure distances in outer space.

If this is a book about time, why worry about distance? Because distance tells us where something exists in any kind of space. You can say that the pillow on your bed is seven feet from the wall with the door, three feet from the wall with the window, and three feet above the floor. That lets anyone know exactly where your pillow is, in space.

Before the 20th century, scientists believed that time and space were two separate things that could never change their measurements—that is, they couldn't stretch, or be compressed. Then a man named Albert Einstein appeared, and shook the world of science. Einstein thought for himself, asking simple questions about the universe we live in and searching for answers through fresh, unbiased eyes. He believed that physical laws must be true everywhere, not just here on Earth. He said that time combines with space to form something called space-time, and that it is not absolute (unchanging) but relative. Einstein's theory of relativity refers to the fact that measurements of distance and time depend on the state of motion of the person doing the measurements.

When you look at a clock, what you really see is light reflected from the face of the clock.
Imagine that you're traveling on that reflection at the speed of light.

As a teenager, Albert Einstein wondered, "What would the world look like if I rode on a beam of light?" Suppose, he thought, a clock in a train station showed a certain time—perhaps 10 hours, 42 minutes, and 14 seconds. And suppose you could leave the station on a train traveling on the same beam of light with which you see the clock, moving at 186,000 miles per second. When you look back at the clock after 1 second, it will still read 10 hours, 42 minutes, and 14 seconds because, according to Einstein's theory of relativity, by traveling at the speed of light, you have cut yourself off from the passage of time.

All working scientists now accept the theory of relativity, which is much more complex than the above example. The scientists have evidence, much of it from experiments with particle accelerators. And recently, two groups of scientists measured emissions from black holes and neutron stars. They found that these massive spinning objects seem to "drag" space-time around with them, as Einstein had predicted.

The faster anything travels, the more slowly time passes for it. In another experiment, a scientist put an atomic clock on the edge of a revolving plate and a second atomic clock at the center. The clock at the edge of the plate kept time more slowly than the clock in the center. When you're on an outside horse on a merry-go-round, you're traveling faster than the person on an inside horse, but your watch is actually running a very, very, very tiny bit slower.

If time can compress, can it run backward as well as forward? Cosmologists—who study the universe and its origins—think that the universe began as a smooth, orderly place, and grew more disordered as it expanded. Scientist Stephen Hawking says that since the arrow of time moves in the direction of disorder, time can only go forward, not backward. If time ran backward, you would remember the future.

Looking Backward into Deep Time

SOME GEOLOGISTS call Earth's earliest eras "deep time." A history of Earth's past can be found in layers of rocks, which record huge changes in life on Earth, as well as dramatic changes in the chemistry of Earth's atmosphere and oceans and totally different arrangements of the continents. An amazing mass extinction, probably caused by the collision of Earth and an asteroid, wiped out the dinosaurs around 65 million years ago. But the dinosaurs dominated the scene only after an even greater extinction—about 250 million years ago—had destroyed as much as 95 percent of the species in the oceans. The fossil record covers less than half of Earth's history. The rest is recorded only in the chemistry and mineralogy of rocks that were formed back then and have survived until today.

Tyrannosaurus Rex

Even though time cannot *go* backward, you can
LOOK BACKWARD INTO DEEP SPACE. If you look at
a star that's 40 light-years away from Earth (40 times
6 trillion miles), its starlight started out 40 years ago,
so you're seeing the star the way it was back then.

Cosmologist Margaret Geller says, "Fortunately for us,
the universe is a time machine. As we look out in space,
we can travel back in time. If we can't figure out how the
universe came to be the way it is, we can actually observe
it with the big telescopes we're building today." Earth's
most powerful telescopes can see back 13 billion
light-years, barely making out the faint light from a
galaxy that formed only a billion years or so after
the start of the universe. Year after year now,
astronomers are able to look backward farther
and farther in time, getting closer to the moment
of the big bang: the creation of the universe.

Scientists keep striving to understand
the beginning moments of time—when
it happened, how it happened, and why.
Newer, larger telescopes search the
heavens for the "first light."

Perhaps, in your lifetime,
they'll find it.

Cosmologist Margaret Geller sees the
beautiful patterns that the universe makes.

On Time
Gloria Skurzynski

THIS BOOK IS FOR
Margaret Geller from
her friend and constant admirer.
— G.S.

PUBLISHED BY
THE NATIONAL GEOGRAPHIC SOCIETY

John M. Fahey, Jr.	*President and Chief Executive Officer*
Gilbert M. Grosvenor	*Chairman of the Board*
Nina D. Hoffman	*Senior Vice President*

PREPARED BY THE BOOK DIVISION

William R. Gray	*Vice President and Director*
Charles Kogod	*Assistant Director*
Barbara A. Payne	*Editorial Director and Editor*
David Griffin	*Design Director*

STAFF FOR THIS BOOK

Nancy Feresten	*Director of Children's Books*
Suzanne Patrick Fonda	*Editor*
Jennifer Emmett	*Associate Editor & Project Editor*
Jo Tunstall	*Editorial Assistant*
Marianne Koszorus	*Design Director of Children's Books*
Suez Kehl Corrado	*Art Director*
Greta Arnold	*Illustrations Editor*
Meredith Wilcox	*Illustrations Assistant*
Deborah E. Patton	*Indexer*
Lewis Bassford	*Production Manager*
Vincent P. Ryan	*Manufacturing Manager*

Copyright © 2000 Gloria Skurzynski. All rights reserved. Reproduction of the whole or any part of the contents without written permission from the publisher is prohibited.

Library of Congress Cataloging-in-Publication Data
Skurzynski, Gloria.
  On time: From seasons to split seconds / by Gloria Skurzynski
     p.   cm.
  Includes index.
Summary: Examines the way humans have measured time throughout history and discusses the various units that are used to keep track of it.
  ISBN 0-7922-7503-9
  1. Time measurements—History Juvenile literature.
[1. Time measurement.] I. Title.
QB209.5.S53 2000
529—dc21   99-33927

Index

Illustrations are indicated by boldface. If illustrations are included within a page span, the entire span is **boldface.**

Acknowledgments

The author is extremely grateful to the following people who gave so generously of their insight and expertise by reviewing this book and suggesting corrections: Dr. Margaret Geller and Dr. Scott Kenyon of the Harvard-Smithsonian Center for Astrophysics; Dr. France Anne Córdova, Vice Chancellor for Research and Professor of Physics, University of California at Santa Barbara; Dr. Jose Wudka, Professor of Physics, University of California at Riverside; Dr. Daniel Mattis, Professor of Physics, University of Utah; Fred McGehan and Don Sullivan of the National Institute of Standards and Technology, Boulder, Colorado; and geologist Genevieve Atwood.

Photo and Illustrations Credits

Dust jacket and art icons, Slim Films; 2–3, Michael Whitehead/Auscape; 4, Buzz Thom, *Track Magazine*; 6–7, Greg Harlin; 8 (both), Michael Yamashita; 8–9, Shusei Nagaoka; 9 (both), Michael Yamashita; 10, Bruce Dale; 11, from *Zoo in the Sky*, by Jacqueline Mitton, illustrated by Christina Balit, published by Frances Lincoln Ltd., © 1998. Reproduced by permission of Frances Lincoln Ltd., 4 Torriano Mews, Torriano Avenue, London NW5 2RZ; 12–13, Kenneth Garrett; 15, Robert Magis; 16–17, Felipe Davalos; 18, Ashmolean Museum, University of Oxford, photo by James L. Stanfield; 19, National Geographic Photographer Jodi Cobb; 20–21, Jerry Lodriguss; 22, Victor Boswell; 23, Corbis-Bettmann; 24, Nathan Benn; 25, SuperStock; 26, Cooper Bridgman Library, National Maritime Museum, Greenwich, England; 28, Richard Olsenius; 28–29, Gil Stimson; 30–31 (both), Shusei Nagaoka; 32, Bruce Dale; 33, courtesy of the National Institute of Standards and Technology; 34, Jean-Leon Huens; 36, Bruce Dale; 37, David Kirshner; 38–39, Graphics by E. Falco and M. Bayuk at National Center for Supercomputing Applications © Smithsonian Astrophysical Observatory, Cambridge, Massachusetts.

The world's largest nonprofit scientific and educational organization, the National Geographic Society was founded in 1888 "for the increase and diffusion of geographic knowledge." Since then it has supported scientific exploration and spread information to its more than nine million members worldwide.

The National Geographic Society educates and inspires millions every day through magazines, books, television programs, videos, maps and atlases, research grants, the National Geography Bee, teacher workshops, and innovative classroom materials.

The Society is supported through membership dues and income from the sale of its educational products. Members receive National Geographic magazine—the Society's official journal—discounts on Society products, and other benefits.

For more information about the National Geographic Society and its educational programs and publications, please call 1-800-NGS-LINE (647-5463), or write to the following address:

National Geographic Society
1145 17th Street N.W.
Washington, D.C. 20036-4688 U.S.A.

Visit the Society's Web site: www.nationalgeographic.com

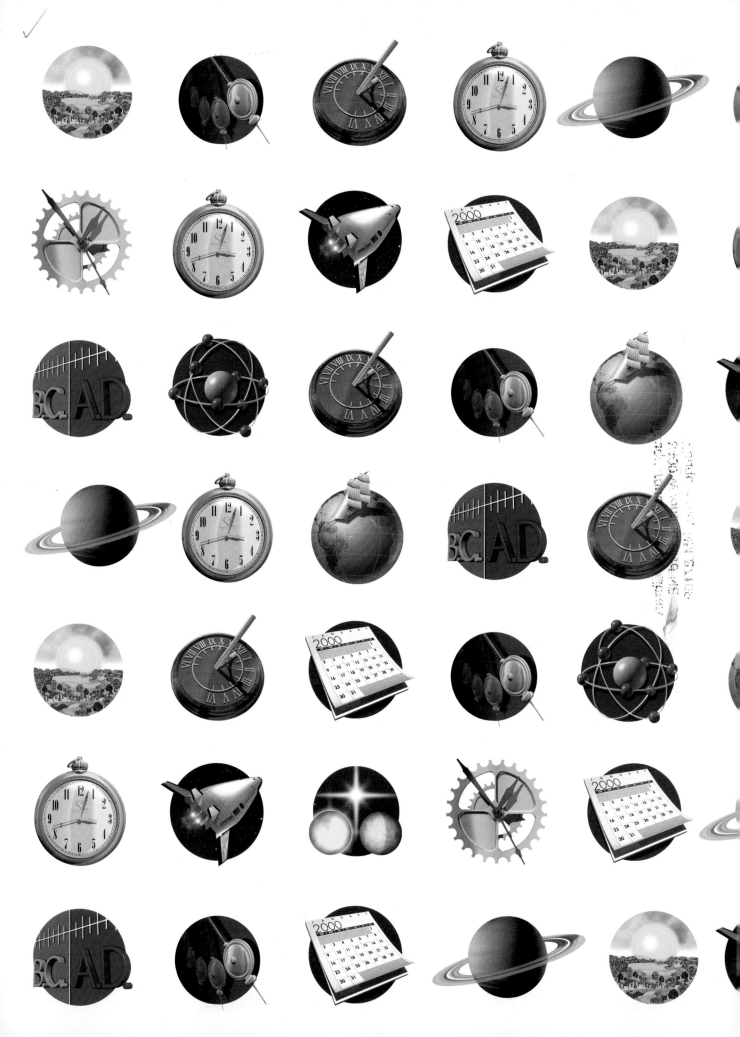